משכן אבלות

Mishkan Aveilut

Where Grief Resides

משכן אבלות
Mishkan Aveilut
Where Grief Resides

EDITOR
Rabbi Eric Weiss

Central Conference of American Rabbis
5779 New York 2019

Library of Congress Cataloging-in-Publication Data
Names: Weiss, Eric, 1956- editor.
Title: Mishkan aveilut : where grief resides / editor, Rabbi Eric
Weiss.
Other titles: At head of cover title: Mishkan aveilut
Description: New York : Central Conference of American Rabbis,
[2019] |
  Includes bibliographical references.
Identifiers: LCCN 2018056800 (print) | LCCN 2018057379 (ebook) |
ISBN 9780881233216 | ISBN 9780881233209 (pbk. : alk. paper)
Subjects: LCSH: Grief--Religious aspects--Judaism. |
Judaism--Liturgy.
Classification: LCC BM645.G74 (ebook) | LCC BM645.G74 M57 2019
(print) | DDC 296.7/6--dc23
LC record available at https://lccn.loc.gov/2018056800

Cover art: Coby's Tallit, copyright © 2017 by Iris Sonnenschein,
www. Irisquilts..com. All rights reserved. Used by permission.

Interior design and typography: Scott-Martin Kosofsky at
  The Philidor Company, Rhinebeck, NY.

IN MEMORY OF
Stanley and Winifred Fried,
Sylvia Glantz,
and Helen Straus.

Dedicated to those in need of healing, and those
who care for them during their trying times.
May they find the support, solace, and comfort they
need and deserve. May one of the prayers, poems,
or readings in this collection speak to those in need.

—*Joanne B. Fried*

Advisory Committee

Rabbi Eric Weiss, Editor
Rabbi Hara Person, Publisher

Rabbi Esther Adler
Rabbi Seth Bernstein, BCC
Rabbi Anna Gray Beroll, BCC
Rabbi Jo Hirschmann, BCC
Rabbi Greg Kanter
Rabbi Elliot Kukla
Rabbi Robert Loewy
Rabbi Edie Meyerson
Rabbi Rex Perlmeter
Rabbi Shira Stern, D. Min., BCC
Rabbi Julia Weisz
Rabbi Marcia Zimmerman

Contents

Grief hurts. Sometimes we can find words to express how we feel; sometimes words are elusive. The content of this book is meant to reflect some of the ways we experience grief: the ways we feel about ourselves, the ways we feel about the person who died, the ways we feel about our community, and the ways we reach for something beyond this world. We hope that however you read this book, you will find something here to give voice to your experience and provide spiritual nourishment. You may agree or disagree with what is written on these pages. You may find something that gives you an insight, a sense of direction, or something that simply affirms your experience. You may find something you want to explore more deeply with someone you trust: a friend, a rabbi, a counselor, or another professional. We encourage you to use what you wish to engage your grief in a way that will support your own journey. Our deepest hope is that what you read here will bring you more deeply into relationship with our common Jewish community.

My child

What do I do?

I miss

My spouse

My parent

My partner

How do I go on?

Where are you no

I thank

My sibling

My family member

My in-law

I hurt

Why didn't you tell me?

My grandchild

My friend

I'm sorry

Bless me

My grandparent   *I pray*

              Talk to me

My neighbor

              I wonder

                        I'm moving on

       I'm forgetting you

    I love   My ex

                        I wish

       My loved one

                   It's hard to remember

My confidante

                   My teacher

    I regret

                   our public figure

         Who would you be now?

Reflections

Reflections

Acknowledgments

TODAH is Hebrew for "Thank you." It shares the same root as the word *hodaah*, "gratitude," found as part of our communal recitation of hopes and dreams in the backbone of our liturgical canon called the *Amidah*. "Thank you" in our tradition recognizes the innate layers of relationship that yield all accomplishment. So too this resource is filled with the constellation of many conversations, dedicated souls, and inspired voices. No one succeeds alone. All spiritual care comes into our communal life from many hearts.

The committee's efforts to shape this work are myriad, from wordsmithing to philosophical comments. *Todah* to Rabbis Esther Adler, Seth Bernstein, Anna Gray Beroll, Jo Hirschmann, Greg Kanter, Elliot Kukla, Robert Loewy, Edie Meyerson, Rex Perlmeter, Shira Stern, Julia Weisz, and Marcia Zimmerman. Thank you also to all the members of the CCAR Worship and Practice Committee, Rabbi Joseph Skoot, Chair, and Rabbis Rebecca Epstein, Nicole Greninger, Lisa Grushcow, Rachel Gurevitz, Dr. Lawrence Hoffman, Yaron Kapitulnik, Tamar Malino, Joel Mosbacher, Joel Sisenwine, Elaine Zecher, and Rabbi Cantor Jeffrey Saxe.

Our movement is at a transition point. For any kind of Judaism, spiritual response must be planted into its terrain so it can choose life. For helping move us forward and for the countless unanticipated moments of rooted growth, thank you to our colleague Rabbi Hara Person. To everyone at the CCAR who helped make this resource a reality, *todah* to Rabbi Steven Fox, and the CCAR Press team, including Sasha Smith, Debbie Smilow, Ortal Bensky, Rabbi Dan Medwin, and Carly Linden. *Todah* also to copyeditor Debra Hirsch Corman and proofreader Michelle Kwitkin-Close.

Much of what led to this book came out of my work at the Bay Area Healing Center. With gratitude, *todah* to the board of the Bay Area Jewish Healing Center: Lenore Bleadon, Ben Bloom, Nancy Boughey, LCSW, Mary DeMay, MD, Marc Dollinger, PhD, Rabbi Sheldon Marder, Susan Moldaw, Gregg Rubenstein, Michelle Tandowsky and Neal Tandowsky, and staff members: Rabbi Natan Fenner, Rabbi Elliot Kukla, Rabbi Jon Sommer, Maxine Epstein, LCSW, and Gail Kolthoff, for their dedication to the field of Jewish spiritual care. A special thank you to Susanna Bensinger, LCSW, Ann Gonski, Abra Greenspan, Zev Hymowitz, Elliot Levin, Lee L. Pollak, LCSW, Ann Lazarus, Phyllis Cook, Joanne Stone, Marsha Guggenheim, Alison Jordan, MFT, Susan Shavin, PhD, Vicky Kelman, and the staff of Grief and Growing™: A Healing Weekend for Individuals and Families in Mourning.

Every hand we hold is connected to every donor. The investment of the wider Bay Area Jewish community, from the singular donor to the legacy commitment, of the Bay Area Jewish Healing Center, has been a vital source of succor that has sustained the often confidential work of grief support. This includes the many endowment and community funds of the Jewish Community Federation and Endowment Fund of San Francisco, the Peninsula, Marin and Sonoma Counties and the Jewish Community Foundation/Jewish Federation of the East Bay. With great tenderness, thank you to every person in grief who trusts the Healing Center with their soul-filled vulnerability.

The interplay between Torah and *kemach* is an ancient one. *Todah* to Joanne Fried, who believed in this book and whose generosity has enabled the mitzvah of bringing this book into the hands of so many in need. And to our colleague Rabbi Robert Loewy, who played an important role in helping the book to come forth, *todah*.

And finally, a speechless *todah* to my husband, Dan.

A Note About Gender

LANGUAGE IS BOTH METAPHOR for what can be ultimately wordless and also the best way we have to communicate with one another. Gender, then, can be both particular and general. As you read these reflections we hope that you will engage them in the gender you prefer. As is the case with original poetry and our Hebrew tradition, gender may be canonized in a way that does not reflect contemporary vision. We encourage you to apply that vision onto any of the reflections in a way that is nourishing to you.

A Note About Grief

THE NATURE OF GRIEF is that it can both numb and stimulate. Grief may render some parts of our life dulled and soft-focused, while other parts of our life become enlivened and magnified. This range of reaction can spiritually align us as we consider the life we have lived and the life we want. All grief encompasses the past, present, and future. This natural reflection can often arise in the ways in which our grief is oriented toward the person who died, the ways in which we encounter community, the inner terrain we explore, and the considerations we have for what is beyond any individual life.

Where we come from, the life we have at any particular moment, and the hopes we have into the future are all natural points of reflection in the midst of loss. Waves of grief may break assumptions, and curiosity may flood forward. The exhaustion of grief may put our body to sleep, and our dreams may awaken our soul. Feelings may burst forth and our words may change a perspective. From the inward to the transcendent, grief often reweaves our lives into a different way of experiencing the world. No matter the particular relationship you had to someone who has died, we hope that the following reflections will be a holistic source of nourishment as you move through the discovery of your grief terrain.

Our culture will always have a current way to understand grief. We will offer medical, psychological, and theological perspectives, yet we know our natural spiritual hunger will draw near to its own sustenance. Grief is universal. It naturally stimulates spiritual reflection and reasonably yearns for a communal response. This collection is designed to complement the anchors our tradition offers to contain, guide, and support grief: *shivah, sh'loshim, yahrzeit,* and *Yizkor.* Those communal foundations of mourning seek to support the personal experience of grief itself. The words on these pages seek to give voice to the personal experience so that we acknowledge the paradox the Rabbis observed millennia ago: because each individual comes to experience grief, it is universal. We hope that the words on these pages will decrease isolation, buoy the spirit, bring clarity to the soul's expression, and invoke a caring community.

Preface

WHEN OUR TEMPLE stood in Jerusalem and was destroyed, the community entered a period of collective grief. In response, the Rabbis began to create a Judaism that would be viable to any contemporary time. The curiosity and imagination of the collective Rabbinic mind took a leap of faith: to contain the caution and fear brought forth at the destruction of the Temple by forming a transportable Jewish life that could live beyond the venue of Jerusalem and move with the people, no matter where they lived. Out of the destruction of the Temple, the Rabbis strived to scaffold a Judaism that through its text study, holiday observance, historical perspective, and guidance for living would create templates for daily life: how to eat, how to conduct business, how to build community, how to teach, how to treat others, how to die, how to mourn, how to stand in Awe.

Out of this context, the Rabbinic imagination crafted a spiritual stance that encompasses the human experience of grief. They declared all mourners be greeted: *HaMakom y'nachem etchem b'toch sh'ar aveilei Tzion virushalayim*, "May the God who comforted the mourners of Zion and Jerusalem comfort you now in your grief." With this, the Rabbis encapsulated the core paradox of grief: grief is a universal human experience, and each of us experiences it unto ourselves. The Rabbinic mind teaches us that for each person, our own grief is as cataclysmic as the destruction of the Temple. Every person's individual loss is linked by the historic arc to the communal loss of our Temple.

This declarative link of historic fact to the inevitable human experience we all come to know binds our communal experience to every individual soul. Its resonance of the inner life with the outer historic experience is a generational vibration across the millennia that catapults us into a future that will forever be linked one generation to the next across time and space. It takes imagination, leaps of faith, curiosity, and the containment of caution to move through one's own grief. Mourning may lead to new ways of seeing, acting, choosing, living. Grief may affirm our faith, it may alter it, it may destroy it, it may leave it untouched. Grief rarely ends a conversation. Rather, grief affirms the thrill and the disappointment of relationship. Death may take a body, but it cannot take a relationship; fraught or healed, relationships often continue after death. We may see our dead, if only in our peripheral vision; we may hear them, if only in memory; we may smell their scent, recall their touch.

Since the destruction of the Temple, our tradition has met each moment by threading our history into the present so that we can wrap ourselves in a fabric that warms the soul. All theology strives to frame our human experience into ritual, prayer, and spiritual reflection. We will never tire of this poetry because it is the endless form with which we express our deepest yearnings. Spiritual reflection—in prayer or ritual—is the form that allows us to link our history to our personal story. This glimpse into moments of life that yearn to be significant, comforting, of solace and succor, follow a path toward wholeness. From the secular to the religious, our natural spiritual hunger seeks nourishment. It is a desire that rises with a demanding vulnerability from the throes of grief and looks all around—inside, outside, and above, for anchor, for firm footing, for the horizon.

This collection, *Mishkan Aveilut: Where Grief Resides*, is an effort to provide the spiritual sustenance we all crave in the midst of one of life's greatest vulnerabilities. Whether grief comes because a loved one died or one is relieved they have left this earth, we are filled with a loss that demands attention. At any moment along the spiritual journey we can be filled with either surety or doubt. We may struggle with language, metaphor, and theology, or we may find them satisfying. Our hope is that the moment you enter into prayerful engagement here, the experience will bequeath you, across the millennia, your place within our people's unbreakable relationship to God, Torah, and Israel. Vulnerability in any endeavor brings the soul's yearnings into new arenas of expression. We hope that this healing book will help weave our human capacity for curiosity into our capacity for spiritual life.

Part I
Building My Tent of Grief

Grief and time have a relationship. If we do not take the time to grieve, then grief will take its time from our day. This discipline to grieve can take many forms: prayer, ritual, or some form of grief schedule will give grief the room it demands. Among the most painful reflections of grief is wondering how to live without the physical presence of the person who has died. Loss pushes us to know that our daily life is not the same. This may bring relief and vitality, or it may bring deprivation and stagnation. It may be the spontaneous burst of energy freed from the confines of relational disappointment. It may be the constricting of activity for lack of knowing how to do something alone. At its core, each day suddenly becomes a leap of faith: to get up, to eat, to move through the day. Living after someone has died takes imagination. Whether from a relationship that began in the womb or a lifetime of adventure into old age, these reflections hope to voice the ways in which grief changes us.

Kavanah

God of All Knowing, I am sometimes speechless, I am sometimes a flood of words. My emotions are a chaotic swirl. Maybe it's like when You were faced with separating Creation day by day. Please help me now as I move through this tumultuous time. Help me find the words I need, help me allow myself the feelings I have, and somehow bring understanding to my grief. Please guide me as I, like You, face the chaos and try to name what is true in the depths of my own soul.

Forgetting Someone

Forgetting someone is like
forgetting to turn off the light in the back yard
so it stays lit all the next day.

But then it's the light
that makes you remember.

       —*Yehuda Amichai*

The Thing Is

to love life, to love it even
when you have no stomach for it
and everything you've held dear
crumbles like burnt paper in your hands,
your throat filled with the silt of it.
When grief sits with you, its tropical heat
thickening the air, heavy as water
more fit for gills than lungs;
when grief weights you like your own flesh
only more of it, an obesity of grief,
you think, *How can a body withstand this?*
Then you hold life like a face
between your palms, a plain face
no charming smile, no violet eyes,
and you say, yes, I will take you
I will love you, again.

—*Ellen Bass*

Grief Arrives in Its Own Time

It doesn't announce itself or knock
on the door of your heart. Suddenly

it's right behind you
looking with great pity

at the back of your neck
and your shoulders on which

it spends days placing a burden
and lifting it. Grief arrives

it its own sweet time, *sweet*
because it lets you know that

you are alive, *time* because
what you are holding becomes

the only day there is: the sun stops
moving, the sky grows utterly quiet

and impossibly blue. Behind the blue
are the stars we can't see and beyond

the stars either dark or light,
both of which are endless.

—*Stuart Kestenbaum*

*!?~

There is no expletive
No hissing consonant-vowel
No bleating scream to say
I miss you:
What happened to your voice that belongs in my ear?
What happened to your hand that belongs in mine?
What happened to all your other parts I've loved?
And where do I belong?

　　　—*Rabbi Eric Weiss*

Talking to Grief

Ah, Grief, I should not treat you
like a homeless dog
who comes to the back door
for a crust, for a meatless bone.
I should trust you.

I should coax you
into the house and give you
your own corner,
a worn mat to lie on,
your own water dish.

You think I don't know you've been living
under my porch.
You long for your real place to be readied
before winter comes. You need
your name,
your collar and tag. You need
the right to warn off intruders,
to consider
my house your own
and me your person
and yourself
my own dog.

                    —*Denise Levertov*

After a Year

Is it an extravagance, this grief?
Is it clean, is it purely itself?
Would I feel it less if he'd been
ready after the treatments
or if he hadn't written
in the black-and-white
speckled notebook I bought him,
"Nothing else to try ... *how, when*?"
What if he had dreamed
death as light on a windowsill,
shorebirds running at a wave?

—*Jennifer Barber*

It makes no sense to say that you are gone,

that I am here. Still. Cool mornings
when the coffee perks as if for you,
when the dogs sigh, when they groan

when the newspaper guy flings the paper
underneath your truck, dead center beneath
your quiet truck with its gas tank still half full,

no sense. Every day mail still arrives for you.
I don't need it all but some I save.
I practice keeping you.

You speak to me soundlessly. Certain
small words in our old good way.
Were we practicing even then

for this? In our quiet times, were we
preparing? Could we have known?
When we were holding hands, then?

—*Janet Winans*

Loss-Change

I don't need spices anymore
The salt drips from my eyes
The apples can keep their core
Mine is already hollowed.

I don't need to refrigerate anymore
Our bed is cold enough
The butter is safe
My heart is already churned.

I don't need the grocer anymore
My stomach has no craving
The earth can keep its bounty
You took mine.

With all we did, why did we never see a desert?
At least you might have taught me to live parched.

—*Rabbi Eric Weiss*

Rent

I stand watch at the dining room window
in my one black dress for the car
to carry us on a journey we dread.
The limo is late and we have to wait
for AAA to come to its rescue and change
a flat. Upstairs my mother sits motionless
at her vanity, the mirror draped in black
though she can peek through a hole
near the bottom and pretend to put on
her face, forbidden as it is.
My father fades even further into the background
since his discovery of the body
in the bathtub on Riverside Drive
his hair suddenly dull and grey as dust
shoulders stooped in what will come to be
his permanent pose. Gone his whistling,
show-tune singing sound track of our lives.
Still on lookout, I see a squirrel
scurry up the Old English Oak
to the bottom branch where I hid from my sister
simply to drive her mad. Perhaps I am to blame
after all for the way she broke apart leaving
pieces of her once-fine mind everywhere I turn.

But what difference does it make? Now it's about
getting through this day and all the ones to follow.
Soon we'll stand in the family room
around a plain pine box, so big
for such a little girl. When the rabbi slits
the black strip of cloth pinned to my dress
I'll feel the knife split me in two and wonder
how I'll learn to make do with what's left.

　　　—*Barbara Leff*

The Widow

I latch the storm door, shunt the cat
down cellar, set the thermostat

and climb twelve steps to go to bed
myself, myself. I fold the spread.

The sheets are crisp. All over town
the yellow mouths of bedrooms yawn

and close on lovers, two by two.
I stuff the noisy door, undo

my buttons, hooks and eyes and stand
back from the mirror. Under hands

that mapped my senses softly as sheep
touch in the fold and turn in sleep

my body turned in appetite.
My jailbird body, long and light,

unfingermarked, unvisited,
grows stupid in the tidy bed.

Now as I turn the clock face down
midnight strikes all over town.

   —*Maxine Kumin*

The Widower

Five winters in a row, my father knuckles
the trunk of his backyard pine
like he's testing a watermelon.
He scolds smooth patches
where bark won't grow,
breaks branches
to find them hollow.
He inhales deeply
and the pine tree has lost
even its scent. He grieves
in trees—my father, the backyard
forest king, the humble
king. The dragging his scepter
through the darkness king.
The wind splits him into shivers.
Rivers of stars
don him like a crown. My king
who won't lay his tenderness down
trembles into the black
unable to stop
his kingdom from dying.
I have failed to quiet
the animal inside him.

If only I would
take his hand.
This man weeping
in the cold,
how quickly I turn
from him.

—*Hafizah Geter*

Trees

When I am sad, when I am pulled tight
into a hardened knot of pain or pity,
I try to find a way to open myself
by thinking of trees. Of course,
it is difficult to think of something so full
and radiant as a tree when I am small
and pulled into a dark closed shell. Sometimes
it is possible only to think of trees
most familiar, trees I have known since childhood:
the willow arching over my earliest memories,
the magnolia of my grandmother's backyard,
the oak that has stood all my life by the edge
    of the road.
Not that it is easy to imagine something rising
    up, tall,
although trees too once were small and knotted
and buried in darkness.

Maybe that is why trees are so comfortable
     in the shadows,
why darkness gathers around them, is drawn to them,
pooling beneath them, collecting on the underside
     of leaves,
between the fingers of their branches. Maybe
that is why trees seek out darkness with their roots,
feeling into the deepest, softest parts of the earth,
to pull from the darkness the sweetness,
and from that sweetness draw the strength
     to look up,
to reach out, to grow towards whatever light
     there might be.

          —*Laura Gilpin*

From Scratch

It's as if everything before
my mother's death, is dying.
As if I have to re-make
everything I've ever known.
All the trees—dogwoods,
magnolias. I have to
give birth to my mother,
my father, my three brothers
take us all back to Memphis,
build the house on Shady Grove
brick by pink brick, paint
the shutters blue. I have to
start the family business, hire
Teenie as head secretary
and the two skinny blondes
who race stock cars after work.
I have to bring the rabbis
from up north, and Jack,
from East Tennessee,
for balance. I have to
send my mother to art school
in the brown convertible,

dirty white top folded back
like a sail, so she can paint
the painting I'm looking at
now, the one from her
Diebenkorn period—no figures,
only fields of blue and green
and around the perimeter
a few graphite lines,
her hand scratching out
a window, a door.

       —*Judy Katz*

October 8th

I follow the past
in the form
of the sound
of my own faded laugh,
barefoot-feet padding
down lanes of broken glass,
running after the flickering lights
of lives that couldn't last.

In this memory,
I catch a glimpse of my father, alive,
and smile at the child
who didn't know he could die.
But my smiling heart begins to hurt
so I turn from this place and leave her behind,
returning to life,
returning to time.

Holding death at arm's length,
we pretend it's unfamiliar.
But if we look a different way,
through death, we see life clearer.

Death follows from the nest.
Holds our hand as we take our last breath.
It is a treble cleft,
defining the high notes;
A Conductor,
for the otherwise tone-deaf.
The ragged figure of destiny
hiding in sight
in the folds of our flesh.
We're *always* on our knees
So I've relearned to breathe
So I can live what is left
of my own fragile breath.

So here I am now, on this one-way street,
marking the point at which now and then meet.
I'll remember for always;
but I'll dance with my grief,
paired up for eternity
with the music left behind
by my father's once-was heartbeat.

—*Sasha Smith*

On a Violent Death

It is difficult to separate the memory from the pain. It hurts to remember, but it is even more frightening to forget. And how easy it is, in this situation, to give in to hate, rage, and the will to avenge.

But I find that every time I am tempted by rage and hate, I immediately feel that I am losing the living contact with my son. Something there is sealed. And I came to my decision, I made my choice. . . .

And I know that within the pain there is also breath, creation, doing good. That grief does not isolate but also connects and strengthens.

—*David Grossman*

When Will I Be Myself Again

"When will I be myself again?"
 Some Tuesday, perhaps,
 In the late afternoon,
 Sitting quietly with a cup of tea
 And a cookie;
 Or Wednesday, same time or later,
 You will stir from a nap and see her;
 You will pick up the phone to call her;
 You will hear her voice—unexpected advice—
 And maybe argue.
 And you will not be frightened,
 And you will not be sad,
 And you will not be alone,
 Not alone at all,
 And your tears will warm you.
 But not today,
 And not tomorrow,
 And not tomorrow's tomorrow,
 But some day,
 Some Tuesday, late in the afternoon,
 Sitting quietly with a cup of tea
 And a cookie
 And you will be yourself again.

—*Rabbi Lewis John Eron*

Practice

Yesterday I practiced
going to the grocery store
to buy milk and eggs.
Today I practice
taking a shower
and waking my children
and feeding them pancakes
and driving them to school.
I practice
listening to the radio
and reading the newspaper
and watching TV.
I practice
going to work
and answering phone calls
and sitting in meetings.
I practice
not averting my eyes from the sadness reflected in
    the eyes of others
as they look at me.

Some of this I know how to do,
Some of this I will learn.
I will practice living without you
until I find some proof
that this could be possible.
I will practice in hopes that one day normal can
   become normal again.

—*Rabbi Melinda Panken*

Dinner for One

Two eggs scrambled, black bean burro
bowl of soup or on occasion, ice cream.
Baked potato, stuffed or virginal, a waffle,
batter saved for breakfast. Slice of pizza,
butter on spaghetti or for a feast, a pair
of lamb chops, rice and frozen spinach.
One expensive artichoke, half kept for
tomorrow, an artichoke with just one heart.
There's the sadness, just one heart.

—*Janet Winans*

My Mother Finds Her Way

Since my father died my mother likes to say, "'Widow' is a harsh word."

She wasn't prepared to be a widow. She was dependent on my father, she was disorganized and shy, and some of her friends wondered how she'd fare. But my mother refused to let his death sideline her. She decided to share her experience of widowhood and write a book—a "how-to" book. How do you start your day? Should you go out with couples? When do you give away the clothes? . . .

She told me not long ago, "Getting into bed alone is the hardest part."

She always was a night owl. My father used to be in bed by nine p.m., calling to her, "Come to bed!" He'd be wearing pressed Brooks Brothers pajamas, and would fall asleep by the time she turned in hours later.

These days when she's up late, she's scrolling through the Web, which she recently learned to use when one of my sons was home from college. She tries to get to bed at what she calls a decent hour. I picture her closing up the house: pulling down the shades, turning off the lights, and finally, climbing into bed.

The next morning, she tells me, she's up early, opening the curtains by her bed, comforted by the roses, remembering how my father would appreciate their

pale pink and yellow beauty when he was in bed his last
few weeks and saw them, as if for the first time. I imagine
her going to her kitchen and remembering she'd better get
to the nursery to pick out a new lemon bush, or make a
list for the dinner party she is planning. There are so many
things she has yet to do.

—*Susan Moldaw*

in the castro

a canon of sobs
runs behind bar music

a father will not be
consoled by his girlfriend
"maybe it was his time"
i hear her say

then join them
in looking through
tinted windows
into the twilight

where death blazes
and flies at us
from every corner
where it was anyway

now the fog comes to lie
like sadness upon us
holds the moon hostage
would lift its mask
if we knew

is this the beginning
of the end or the end
of what's just begun
or the end of the end

we don't want to know
what we can't fathom
unless we are merged with it

each day pushes us
closer to the wheel
our grief keeps on
carving fresh and stronger
spirit from the shipwreck
of callous couplings

piled like debris
upon our past

—*John Selby*

Twenty-two Years Later

I was talking to our close friend
also a pilot and asked him did we
ever find out exactly how, and
having inspected the wreckage
he said you just made a mistake
that maybe you hadn't gotten much
sleep the night before and in the
long pre-dawn dark you hadn't
climbed to the right altitude so
when the earth came up before
the plane and here he illustrated
with his hands one hand as the plane
gliding forward one as the terrain
gradually rising up in a wall his
fingertips lightly touching his palm
like a gentle sign for time out
and you didn't see it, that's how:
instantly. I felt a massive subtraction
from my personal mountain of
sorrow because for all these years
I imagined you flying terribly high
when suddenly you couldn't see
through the Arctic dark which
way was up I even pictured your
to-go cup spilling your twisted

expression as the plane started free
falling and you kept trying to
right it and worst there was a then when
you knew you couldn't and that
moment has been the absolute seat
the capital of my grief because
you were alone with the mail
for the Inuit villages still un-
delivered and now I think well
this will be the strangest, very
strangest good news of both our lives.

—*Jessica Greenbaum*

My Dead

"Only the dead don't die" Y.S.K.

Only they are left me, they are faithful still
whom death's sharpest knife can no longer kill.

At the turn of the highway, at the close of day
they silently surround me, they quietly go my way.

A true pact is ours, a tie time cannot dissever.
Only what I have lost is what I possess forever.

        —Ra'hel

Love Knows No Shame

Love knows no shame. To be loving is to be open to grief, to be touched by sorrow, even sorrow that is unending. The way we grieve is informed by whether we know love. Since loving lets us let go of so much fear, it also guides our grief. When we lose someone we love, we can grieve without shame. Given that commitment is an important aspect of love, we who love know we must sustain ties in life and death. Our mourning, our letting ourselves grieve over the loss of loved ones is an expression of our commitment, a form of communication and communion. Knowing this, and processing the courage to claim our grief as an expression of love's passion does not make the process simple in a culture that would deny us the emotional alchemy of grief. Much of our cultural suspicion of intense grief is rooted in the fear that the unleashing of such passion will overtake us and keep us from life. However, this fear is usually misguided. In its deepest sense, grief is a burning of the heart, an intense heat that gives us solace and release. When we deny the full expression of our grief, it lays like a weight on our hearts, causing emotional pain and physical ailments. Grief is most often unrelenting when individuals are not reconciled to the reality of loss.

Love invites us to grieve for the dead as ritual of mourning and as celebration. As we speak our hearts in mourning we share our intimate knowledge of the dead, of who they were and how they lived. We honor their presence by naming the legacies they leave us. We need not contain grief when we use it as a means to intensify our love for the dead and dying, for those who remain alive.

—*bell hooks*

יָגַעְתִּי בְקָרְאִי נִחַר גְּרוֹנִי.

I am weary with calling; my throat is dry.

Psalm 69:4

Part II

Living Without You in a Tent of Grief

Grief is that spontaneous reach for the telephone before remembering that the person you want to call will not answer the phone. We come to know the nature of loss by what we miss: a particular touch, a tone of voice, a look. Our bodies can crave the heat of someone next to us, our minds can crave how someone's thought process could imagine something anew, our feelings can crave the satisfaction of affirmation. We face an emptiness: the future that will not evolve, the satisfaction that will never come, yearning that will never be realized. Grief moves a relationship from this world into something else. We may be anxious for another moment of wholeness, we may be relieved from an endless striving. Grief can be clarifying of relationship because relationships can continue after death or they can rest forever silent.

Kavanah

God of Relationship, when I think of the one who has died, I wonder what it might be like to have one more conversation, one more embrace, to maybe even understand something more clearly. Just as my relationship with You has had many parts, I hope that my grief will reveal more deeply all the ways in which relationships with others can bring me even closer to knowing the yearnings of my soul.

When a Man Dies

When a man dies, they say "He was gathered unto
    his fathers."
As long as he is alive, his fathers are gathered
    within him,
each cell of his body and soul a delegate from one
    of his
thousands of fathers since the beginning of time.

      —Yehuda Amichai

The Weight of Absence

When you died our house sank deeper into the earth,
pressing on the roots of trees.
I could feel it sinking
as each visitor pushed open the front door,
laden with cakes and casseroles, the full weight
of their bodies—every muscle and tendon,
shinbone   pelvis   hips   moving
down the hallway, moving past the closet
where your dresses hung, still with your smell,
moving into the living room where our father
sat low to the ground.

I had watched you grow smaller and smaller,
ice chips on your tongue.
And as the morphine took you
here and there, Paris and summer camp,
the lake at night—
I thought I understood:
lighter and lighter
you would become,
a lightness leading
to nothing.

But the house did not rise that day;
it sank.
No mass   no matter
no thing   in the bed
in the blankets
in your place.

—*Judy Katz*

"I have planted you in my garden . . ."

I have planted you in my garden,
in my heart that cannot sleep.
Your boughs grow entangled in it
and in it your roots strike deep.

There is no rest and no quiet
in my garden all day long.
It is you in it, you in it singing
amidst flutter of wing and song.

— *Ra'hel*

Separation

Your absence has gone through me
Like thread through a needle.
Everything I do is stitched with its color.

—*W. S. Merwin*

The World Series: For My Father

While machines flashed red numerals
hope, despair, hope
your long graceful fingers
reached up from your ICU-induced sleep state
to trace figures in airborne columns of debits and credits.

Yiddish was your first language
but numbers were your native tongue.
Balance sheets spoke to you of nuance,
challenges mastered and tamed,
the stories and dramas of the universe.

Numbers talked
and you answered.
You wrote your life story in their epic language
of plusses and minuses.

Ebbetts Field was your princely realm,
a boyhood kingdom in which
the beauty and order of stats
kept the chaos away.

Peppy they called you in high school
because Pepsi's kept you sharp.
The reliable math of poker and
the clean geometry of pool sharking
provided cool cash
stored always in serial number order.

Becoming an accountant
provided an arithmetic solution
to the sum of your first generation yearnings.
Controlling the figures in ledgers and spread sheets
supplied the way to amount
to a man of substance.

You would have loved tonight's game,
a four-of-four sweep for my son's team.
As we watched, his eyes on the screen and my eyes
   on him,
he held forth in that language of
stats and averages, innings and outs,
that I haven't heard since your numbers went still.

—*Rabbi Hara E. Person*

Ever

Never, never, never, never, never.
—King Lear

Even now I can't grasp "nothing" or "never."
They're unholdable, unglobable, no map to nothing.
Never? Never ever again to see you?
An error, I aver. You're never nothing,
because nothing's not a thing.
I know death is absolute, forever,
the guillotine—gutting—never to which we
   never say goodbye.
But even as I think "forever" it goes "ever"
and "ever" and "ever." *Ever after.*
I'm a thing that keeps on thinking. So *I never see you*
is not a thing or think my mouth can ever. Aver:
You're not "nothing." But neither are you something.
Will I ever really *get* never?
You're gone. Nothing, never—ever.

—*Meghan O'Rourke*

First night in the grave

It's cold the first night in the grave,
the snow falling,
the body just starting to understand.

The snow is falling
and the spirit wanders
back and forth
from here to there,
just starting to understand.

I want to translate this poem into German,
a solemn language,
a language I don't understand.
I think it will be a small comfort to me
in a language I don't understand.

I am missing you tonight
with the snow falling,
your first night in the grave.

       —*Merle Feld*

I needed to talk to my sister . . .

I needed to talk to my sister
talk to her on the telephone   I mean
just as I used to every morning
in the evening too whenever the
grandchildren said a sentence that
clasped both our hearts

I called   her phone rang four times
you can imagine my breath stopped   then
there was a terrible telephonic noise
a voice said   this number is no
longer in use   how wonderful I
thought   I can
call again they have not yet assigned
her number to another person despite
two years of absence due to death

—Grace Paley

Prayer for the Dead

The light snow started late last night and continued
all night long while I slept and could hear it
    occasionally
enter my sleep, where I dreamed my brother
was alive again and possessing the beauty of youth,
    aware
that he would be leaving again shortly and that is
    the lesson
of the snow falling and of the seeds of death that are
    in everything
that is born: we are here for a moment
of a story that is longer than all of us and few of us
remember, the wind is blowing out of someplace
we don't know, and each moment contains rhythms
within rhythms, and if you discover some old piece
of your own writing, or an old photograph,
you may not remember that it was you and even if it
    was once you,
it's not you now, not this moment that the synapses fire
and your hands move to cover your face in a gesture
of grief and remembrance.

    —*Stuart Kestenbaum*

Birthday, No More

This empty space in time,
In my heart,
Is yours.
It is the space for yearning,
The space of memory,
The day your light came into the world.
A day of sorrow for what was lost,
Birthdays that will never be.

This day touches
The depths of my grief and loss.
This day touches
A wound and makes it new.

God of generations,
Be with me
As we remember what was
And what might have been.

I miss you.

—Alden Solovy

Shiva

Back at my mother's
the ladies help themselves
to the traditional spread of bagels
and lox, white fish and herring
displayed on the deco table cloth,
her embossed monogram
etched as well into the stemware
in the mahogany breakfront,
the ornate key missing in action.

In search of the will prior to the service
I pried open the fold-out escritoire
found only scrapes and scratches
from my Roy Rogers cap gun
before the insistent scent of my father's cigars
sent me back to Valentine Avenue
where my sister and I played
ring toss with the wooden torso
still sitting on the bottom shelf.

Now the ladies laugh as someone
remembers the time my mother
smashed her sister-in-law's cherished
crystal on the kitchen floor
as only Florence could
while I imagine the breakfront invade
my San Francisco flat
where I fled after my sister's death.

Now there's only me to divvy
up the spoils, decide what will stay
and what will go, all the while
telling myself it's only stuff
even as the tears begin to flow.

—*Barbara Leff*

Left behind

Surely you departed by mistake.
You would not have gone without goodbye,
so much still to do. Orderly in ways that mattered,
people ways, not bound by things.

Our garage a jumble—tents, cast ironware,
scorched coffee pots, a toolbox which can't close
on your stuff and your father's.

Your desktop littered—card, notes, receipts,
awards you never cherished, simply kept.

A dresser drawer of albums, baby books, photos
not identified, pieces of stories lost. You left too soon.

The bed of your truck unswept, red phone light blinking
unheard calls. At your place the cup of tea you started.
I have the dense white mug, tea-stained.

So. On winter Sundays now at dusk, as shadows lengthen
we attend. Left behind, it's true, and yet the fabric holds.
Invisible, unbreakable, what was and what remains.

—*Janet Winans*

The Death of a Parent

Move to the front
of the line
a voice says, and suddenly
there is nobody
left standing between you
and the world, to take
the first blows
on their shoulders.
This is the place in books
where part one ends, and part two begins,
and there is no part three.
The slate is wiped
not clean but like a canvas
painted over in white
so that a whole new landscape
must be started,
bits of the old still showing underneath—
those colors sadness lends
to a certain hour of evening.

Now the line of light
at the horizon
is the hinge between earth
and heaven, only visible
a few moments
as the sun drops
its rusted padlock
into place.

—*Linda Pastan*

After a Sudden Death

It happened so fast.
You were here. Now gone.
We had joy. Now loss.
We celebrated. Now we mourn.

How fragile is each breath?
How uncertain is each hour?
How precious is each day?
How brief is one life?

Oh, to still be with you
In this beauty and wonder.
Oh, to hear your voice,
To hold your hand,
To sit beside you.

—Alden Solovy

The Life of Memory

Robert's wife had died, and he couldn't sleep. His friends suggested he take sleeping pills. In a moment of quiet reflection, I asked him which side of the bed he was sleeping on.

"I'm sleeping on my own side," he said.

"What is on your wife's side?" I asked.

"Newspapers, books, anything. I try to read until I'm so exhausted I can't keep my eyes open and feel like I'm going to just collapse, but it doesn't really work. The night is the hardest time. I miss her the most then. I can't settle down, so I just lie awake, exhausted, in a state of agitation."

"Try sleeping on your wife's side of the bed."

It's purely anecdotal. There isn't any scientific research to prove it. But it seems that when their wives die, men in grief can sleep better when they sleep where their wives slept.

Sarah had lost her husband. "I can't sleep," she said. "I miss him so much at night. I can get through the day just putting one foot in front of the other, but I collapse exhausted into bed and just stare into the dark. And I just can't bring myself to clean out his things. Every time I do, I just end up holding his shirts and smelling them."

When Sarah started to sleep in her husband's t-shirt, she began to sleep through the night.

This sleeplessness experience is not exclusive to grieving husbands and wives. It occurs within the context of any close relationship. The truth is that all relationships continue after death. . . . Death may take away a body, but it cannot take away a memory, a hope for the future, a voice, a smell, a touch. Those belong to life. Death may leave us lonely, but it cannot take away a relationship. That belongs to the living, forever.

—Rabbi Eric Weiss

Thirty Days of August

How did it come to pass
that our six children,
huddled together in a tight
circle of fear,
threw handfuls of the crumbling
earth upon your coffin?

Did the rabbi's Aramaic *Yisgadal
Veyiskadash* comfort you
and the God of Abraham
give you solace?
Did long nights of sleep
cradle you, or was this
Aramaic tongue a magic
incantation to bring
you back to me,
to our six children
standing here in shocked
silence?

And it came to pass
that on the thirty-first day of August,
in torpid summer heat
the telephone rang
to break the silence.
A faint voice, slowly intoned
your death, and I stood
alone.

I came to gather the remnants
of your life: wallet, glasses, pipe,
worn tweed jacket, manuscript
unfinished, letters held by a
fraying string that bound
us together.

Why does this bed still bear
the curve of circling body,
embrace of pillow,
scent of pipe, troubled
sleep that bears you
toward me everywhere?

—*Shulamith Chernoff*

My Body

In sleep
you wrap your body
around me
holding me against you,
pressing your warmth
into my back,
your hand cupping my breast
defining my shape.
I could sleep like this forever.

But you are gone and
my back doesn't know
where it is.
My breast, splayed out
on the bed sheet,
has lost its form,
my body, decoupled,
floats sleeplessly
untethered.

—*Carol Allen*

Epitaph

Tell him this: she couldn't forgive herself
for her dark depressions.
She walked through her life
with apologetic steps.

Tell that until her death
she faithfully guarded the fire
entrusted to her, with pure hands,
and is burning in that same fire.

How in her hours of bravado
she battled hard with God,
how deeply her blood sang,
and how lightweights destroyed her.

—*Anna Margolin*

Anniversary of Death

Forsaking and confessing. Walking and stumbling
   again.
O, mother, how hard it is for me.

The breath, from your own you put into me, many
   years ago,
was a raw deal,
I know:

the pity was greater than I was allowed
and the times were tenfold harder than I could bear.

Maybe another man, born to a different woman,
would somehow have managed to make his way in
   the darkness.
For me it wasn't possible.

Almost all the conditional clauses are gone with
   the wind
and a great regret has left its traces.

Most of the sage advice given me wasn't worth a damn.
I know now it's a matter of character
given by your spirit.
That's why it's lost to me.

"Listen to Uncle," I heard, TAKE IT EASY.
I did try I did, but nothing worked out.
My love was harsher and stronger than usual.
Even the silences turned state's evidence.

I've been so happy, don't fret about me,
Here and there I've even been of some use.

Rest in peace next to the man whose half flows in me.
You saw the dark unseen side of the moon.

     —Haim Gouri

Remembered

My father died suddenly
in the thickness of life
appointments in his calendar
emails unread
new pants still waiting for the tailor.
Standing room only at his funeral,
the hall crammed with admirers, colleagues,
    boyhood friends.
During *shiva* he was remembered
in all the textures of his days.

My grandmother died slowly
over several years
her incremental vanishing
noted only in retrospect.
She outlived her past
and is remembered only in brittle shards.

—*Rabbi Hara E. Person*

On Losing a Baby

In this world of endless possibilities,
Some things are not to be,
A voiceless answer to my prayers,
An echo of the sounds of creation
A tree uprooted then replanted
The sun tracing a path backward
Across the vast hollow horizon.

Some things are not to be,
The baby that grew tenderly within
Gone now, leaving whispers and flutters
A trail of tears, a mountain-top
Loneliness
Born from wind, salt and clay.

The body remembers with neural connections
Woven together to embrace me,
Remind me
You were once here
A frail silvery thread connected
You ever so tentatively to me.

It frayed as the twilight unfolded
The world of endless possibilities
Offered one more thing, not to be:
This loss I wanted to refuse,
The silver thread needs mending
Frail yes, but you were once here.

Not in full form, not in full color
Not full of spirit nor body
And yet something of you lingers.
You belong in the twilight,
You dwell in the whispers,
You echo in my holy tears.

—*Rabbi Hanna Yerushalami*

Loss of a Young Child

My God:
Have you seen him yet?
Do you cradle her as only I can?
Will you please teach him how to speak so that one day
I can hear his voice?
In the meantime, please tuck them in tightly, will you?

—*Rabbi Eric Weiss*

Your Death Is Not a Onetime Event

Your death was not a onetime event,
like a tornado or a bad first date
that harden into memory the minute they're over.

No, you die over and over, every day, in more ways
than I can count.
It happens when I expect it and especially when I
don't.

I lose you all over again when I eat a salad with tangy
blue cheese dressing or a bowl of cold borscht, and
when I notice the nubby knit of an argyle sweater
vest, and when I hear the buzzing of a Cessna
kissing the clouds beneath a blue sky, and when
something makes me laugh and I think you would
have laughed too.

I lose you again on birthdays and anniversaries, when
your dependable, sweet call never comes, no matter
how much I expect it.

I lose you at Passover, when your bowls and bowls of
charoset from around the world are missing from
the table, and now there will never be enough
charoset on the table ever again.

I will lose you again and again, when your children get
   married, and my children become bar and bat mitzvah,
   and your grandchildren are born and you can't hold
   them, and love them, and make them laugh.

You are so absent now where you were always present,
   and your death isn't in the past.
It happens over and over again, every day, in ways both
   tiny and enormous.
You keep dying, and I keep grieving.

   —*Rabbi Melinda Panken*

Another Country

> *Yea though I walk through the valley of the*
> *shadow of death . . .*
> —Psalm 23

Five months to the day
after her husband died
my friend saw him
emerge from the Starbucks
across the street.
She ran through traffic
to reach him and screamed
his name but—as in a bad dream—
the faster she ran
the further ahead he got
until she lost sight of him
leaned against a lamppost
and slithered onto the sidewalk
her being, the embodiment
of a sob.

She doesn't recall
how she got home
but relays the difficulty
of crossing the park
thick with groundhog holes
she'd never noticed

and willows weeping
conspicuously.
It's not safe she repeats
a refrain I fear
I'll hear again and again.

I imagine her wandering
a wasteland of craggy surfaces
each step a test of balance
as she stares straight ahead
a footfall away from toppling.

I force my focus back to her face
her eyes move across a landscape
at once familiar and foreign
and I fight hard to keep still
allow her to learn
the lay of the land.

—*Barbara Leff*

Kaddish

Strange now to think of you, gone without corsets &
   eyes, while I walk on the sunny pavement of Green-
   wich Village.
downtown Manhattan, clear winter noon, and I've been
   up all night, talking, talking, reading the Kaddish
   aloud, listening to Ray Charles blues shout blind on
   the   phonograph
the rhythm the rhythm—and your memory in my head
   three years after—And read Adonais' last triumphant
   stanzas aloud—wept, realizing how we suffer—
And how Death is that remedy all singers dream of, sing,
   remember, prophesy as in the Hebrew Anthem, or
   the Buddhist Book of Answers—and my own imagination
   of a withered leaf—at dawn—

   —*Allen Ginsberg*

On the Home Front

That day when he held her and said
oh, *now* what are we going to do
and she said, we'll deal,
we'll deal with it,
she knew Deal could act elusive
and at times deceptive
but she left the word dangling, mid-air

Deal moved in and hung over them with its smug smile,
waiting for an executive decision
or a semblance of a game plan.
But within weeks, narcissist that it is,
Deal got bored, felt underused
and quickly ran off,
looking for action elsewhere.

That's when Coping arrived, empty-handed.
It floated through the house limply,
struggling on its own, leaving them
with no words to cling to,
serving up spineless Hope
first to one then to the other.
It was not enough.

At last Surrender marched in and
kicked Coping aside.
It secured its position and
tidied up the mess,
taking control those last few days,
giving comfort when it could
to her and finally to him

Later it lingered in the house,
gathered up all the desperate words
that had been left hanging,
I love you, I'm here with you, and
tucked them away for safe-keeping
knowing they would be needed some day.
It slipped away unnoticed.

—*Carol Allen*

For the Record

After the funeral, Peggy sent a note.
She'd heard you "made your get-away"—
as if you'd thrown a few things in a bag
and off to the next world.
But she didn't see our father rocking
those last hours in the corner of the bedroom.
Or Aaron and me marooned
on the bed with you.
She must not have heard about
the visiting nurse we knew ten days
and trusted more than medicine or blood,
the one who said hearing is the last sense to go
and we believed her, and spoke to you
like midwives at a birth: *Relax*, we said
to your laboring body. *It's okay.*

What can I say—it's trouble getting in
and trouble getting out.
I've seen it both ways.
Is this where I tell you? Sometimes
your absence is a brightly lit field
I am lying in, back against the earth,
afternoon sun warming my face.
Sometimes the wide open space of you gone
is all it takes to let the whole world in.

—*Judy Katz*

One Evening, Years Later

I see the body of my mother over the horizon
expansive finally as sky, a giant
Henry Moore-like figure stretching out
in cloud. No, more like Matisse—languorous,
reclining, arms thrown overhead. I've never seen her
so relaxed. She is done with bones and clothes,
her breasts her own, her belly floating. She is like a
woman
who's had her way with the world and rolled over
for a final cigarette in the blue
of the not-world—

        and the earth itself,
small and complete beside her. As if
she gave birth to it. As if
it will be fine without her.

     —Judy Katz

Hard Mournings

Mornings are the toughest,
That between time
When I'm not quite awake,
When my mind settles
Back to the familiarity and
The certainty of you.
Until I remember your passing.
Hard mornings,
Hard mournings,
Blend into evenings
Of solitude and sorrow.

Perhaps I'm wrong.
Evenings are the problem,
When the quiet crushes my breath
And the growing darkness
Shadows my heart
Until blessed sleep
Descends from heaven.

Mornings are the toughest
New beginnings,
Each day an echo of loss.
Evenings are the roughest reminders
Of your absence.
Each night a hollow silence,
Emptiness in the space you once held.

—*Alden Solovy*

The Scent of Grief

Why is this so hard?
Anticipating this moment, I spent years
in therapists' offices sniffing out insights,
planting my own seeds, and tending them
like an earlier ancestor making a desert bloom.
Also over coffee with friends I grew
to anticipate relief as if the scent of reconciliation
wafted
from an exotic flower toward this eventual day.
Now it is here
like a long awaited ship returned from war celebrating
    the peace.
And I am so damn sad.

Over the years, inhaling the fragrance of a new garden,
when so many said: "You've already grieved,"
"How could you grieve anything you've never had?"
    I thought:
I will be free then, able to really move into my life,
unfettered by hope they'll show up, even apologize.
And so I picked my flowers ending
each week breathing in my week's accomplishments.
Then I got a call, and flew to the graveside dutifully
like a wounded soldier limping up the family walk-way,
    hobbling.
And I am so damn sad.

I took so many walks that left the scent of fields at
    my ankles,
and gave me stamina to write letters, never mailed,
but read aloud with panting tears to surrogates then
ripped and buried into soil that left the aroma of new
    life under my fingernails.
Now the day is here
like the negotiated quiet of surrender in the once
    bomb-shouting night.
And I am so damn sad.

How is it that you can fight so hard for your life to just
    enjoy a cup of coffee,
Its fragrant elixir, to wake up;
And still grieve at this eventual day? Now it is here:
We don't grieve because we have loved; that it turns
    out is a half-truth.
We grieve because it is in the soil of humanity; we are
    created from it,
humus to our species, in our nature
to recognize something gone away,
to sniff it like a loyal dog at the graveyard, to know
    the scent
like a wild animal marking safety,
or tribal scout lighting a fire wafting its protective
    plume,
so we can sleep before the next sunrise.

—*Rabbi Eric Weiss*

הַשְׁכִּיבֵֽנוּ, יְיָ אֱלֹהֵֽינוּ, לְשָׁלוֹם,
וּפְרֹשׁ עָלֵֽינוּ סֻכַּת שְׁלוֹמֶֽךָ.

Give me a place to rest,
spread over me a shelter of peace.

Adapted from *Hashkiveinu, Mishkan T'filah*

Part III
Widening Our Tent of Grief

Grief interaction can be awkward. We trip over language. We are clumsy. The outside world can seem distant, a whirlwind, unwelcoming. It can also be a place of solace; to be happily lost in a crowd, distracted, or passive. The work of reestablishing social interaction, exploring new ways of being in relationship, or taking a leap of faith—all of these can be a source of discovery or a source of isolation. Grief can bid us to take the leap of faith to continue life even after loss. Grief can propel us into a community that we can help to form, a community that can become better at grief-growth.

Kavanah

God of Tikkun, the way I see others and the way others see me is different now. I find I now re-form relationships. What an awesome task. It is as if I am a Child of Israel anew, wandering in a place that is both familiar and strange at the same time. As I cross new paths, as I walk aimlessly, as I cry out and sing with relief, please guide me, please feed me. I do not know the place where I will arrive, but in my leap of faith, please give me a safe landing.

An Eternal Window

In a garden I once heard
a song or an ancient blessing.

And above the dark trees
a window is always lit, in memory

of the face that looked out of it,
and that face too

was in memory of another
lit window.

—*Yehuda Amichai*

Please Ask

Someone asked me about you today.
It's been so long since anybody has done that.
It felt so good to talk about you,
To share my memories of you,
To simply say your name out loud.
She asked me if I minded talking about
What happened to you . . .
Or would it be too painful to speak of it.
I told her I think of it every day
And speaking about it helps me to release
The tormented thoughts whirling around in my head.
She said she never realized the pain
Would last this long . . .
She apologized for not asking sooner.
I told her, "Thanks for asking."
I don't know if it was curiosity
Or concern that made her ask,
But I told her, "Please do it again sometime . . .
Soon."

—*Barbara Taylor Hudson*

Time Does Not Bring Relief

Time does not bring relief; you all have lied
Who told me time would ease me of my pain!
I miss him in the weeping of the rain;
I want him at the shrinking of the tide;
The old snows melt from every mountain-side,
And last year's leaves are smoke in every lane;
But last year's bitter loving must remain
Heaped on my heart, and my old thoughts abide.
There are a hundred places where I fear
To go,—so with his memory they brim.
And entering with relief some quiet place
Where never fell his foot or shone his face
I say, "There is no memory of him here!"
And so stand stricken, so remembering him.

—*Edna St. Vincent Millay*

Shock

Your heart is breaking—
and they offer you clichés.

You see, they are frightened, too.
They feel threatened and ill at ease.
But they are sharing as best
they can.

Accept their companionship,
but you need not take their advice.

You may simply say, "Thank you
for coming."

And then do what is best for
you.

    —Rabbi Earl Grollman

Grief's Slow Wisdom

The melody that the loved one played upon the piano of our life will never be played quite that way again, but we must not close the keyboard and allow the instrument to gather dust. We must seek out other artists of the spirit, new friends who gradually will help us to find the road to life again, who will walk that road with us.

—Rabbi Joshua Loth Liebman

Present

Dying is the way we make room for the next iteration
of humanity.

—Mary G. DeMay, M.D.

What if the life they lived was good enough just because
they woke up every morning?
What if the life she lived was just fine because she
breathed all those years?
What if the Sake of it was for Evolution: One leap of faith
whose meaning is yet
To be discovered, whose purpose is not the point but
rather: What if as is
My grief was not a stage but just a contribution: To all
who have come before me to all
Those who will come after me, just like standing in line
for the bus just hoping
To get a window seat so I could share what I saw. What if
my grief was just another invitation, there have been
So many, to just join our common humanity? And I said
Yes.

—Rabbi Eric Weiss

Try to Praise the Mutilated World

Try to praise the mutilated world.
Remember June's long days,
and wild strawberries, drops of rosé wine.
The nettles that methodically overgrow
the abandoned homesteads of exiles.
You must praise the mutilated world.
You watched the stylish yachts and ships;
one of them had a long trip ahead of it,
while salty oblivion awaited others.
You've seen the refugees going nowhere,
you've heard the executioners sing joyfully.
You should praise the mutilated world.
Remember the moments when we were together
in a white room and the curtain fluttered.
Return in thought to the concert where music flared.
You gathered acorns in the park in autumn
and leaves eddied over the earth's scars.
Praise the mutilated world
and the gray feather a thrush lost,
and the gentle light that strays and vanishes
and returns.

—*Adam Zagajewski*

The Names

Yesterday, I lay awake in the palm of the night.
A soft rain stole in, unhelped by any breeze,
And when I saw the silver glaze on the windows,
I started with A, with Ackerman, as it happened,
Then Baxter and Calabro,
Davis and Eberling, names falling into place
As droplets fell through the dark.

Names printed on the ceiling of the night.
Names slipping around a watery bend.
Twenty-six willows on the banks of a stream.

In the morning, I walked out barefoot
Among thousands of flowers
Heavy with dew like the eyes of tears,
And each had a name—
Fiori inscribed on a yellow petal
Then Gonzalez and Han, Ishikawa and Jenkins.

Names written in the air
And stitched into the cloth of the day.
A name under a photograph taped to a mailbox.
Monogram on a torn shirt,
I see you spelled out on storefront windows
And on the bright unfurled awnings of this city.
I say the syllables as I turn a corner —

Kelly and Lee,
Medina, Nardella, and O'Connor.

When I peer into the woods,
I see a thick tangle where letters are hidden
As in a puzzle concocted for children.
Parker and Quigley in the twigs of an ash,
Rizzo, Schubert, Torres, and Upton,
Secrets in the boughs of an ancient maple.

Names written in the pale sky.
Names rising in the updraft amid buildings.
Names silent in stone
Or cried out behind a door.
Names blown over the earth and out to sea.

In the evening—weakening light, the last swallows.
A boy on a lake lifts his oars.
A woman by a window puts a match to a candle,
And the names are outlined on the rose clouds—
Vanacore and Wallace,
(let X stand, if it can, for the ones unfound)
Then Young and Ziminsky, the final jolt of Z.
Names etched on the head of a pin.
One name spanning a bridge, another undergoing
    a tunnel.
A blue name needled into the skin.

Names of citizens, workers, mothers and fathers,
The bright-eyed daughter, the quick son.
Alphabet of names in a green field.
Names in the small tracks of birds.
Names lifted from a hat
Or balanced on the tip of the tongue.
Names wheeled into the dim warehouse of memory.
So many names, there is barely room on the walls of
the heart.

   —*Billy Collins*

All the Names We Will Not Know

Before dawn, trembling in air down to the old river,
circulating gently as a new season
delicate still in its softness, rustling raiment
of hopes never stitched tightly enough to any hour.
I was almost, maybe, just about, going to do that.
A girl's thick dark hair, brushed over one shoulder
so regularly no one could imagine it not being there.
Hair as a monument. Hovering—pitched.
Beloved sister, maker of plans, main branch,
we needed you desperately, where have you gone?
Here is the sentence called No no no no no.
Come back, everything grants you your freedom,
here in the mire of too much thinking,
we drown, we drown, split by your echo.

—*Naomi Shihab Nye*

Stones

At Normandy

Endless rows of white crosses
recall the wineries back home:
vines planted at precise intervals
to insure maximum yield.
Here where there's neither
crop nor profit,
precision gives way to prayer.
Symmetry shifts to surprise:
a single six-sided star
then another, and yet another, scattered
like punctuation marks in a run-on sentence:
a pause to underscore the waste of war.
Without words, we scavenge for stones
spread out to pay respects.
I place a pebble on the grave of one
who at 22 saw things I don't dare imagine,
his name as familiar as my own—
a distant cousin perhaps, or not—
just a soul, like any other, gone
from this earth the length of a lifetime.

I hold tight to the stones
as the grass moves in waves
ripples and curls at the sandy
edge of each gravestone
each part of a unique eco-system
whose journey will continue
long past the end of mine.

—Author Unknown

Tisha B'Av

Together we sit on the ground
and mourn for the peace of Jerusalem,
like the treasure we each wanted-
we pulled and we pulled,
you pulled and I pulled,
and yes, of course,
finally we succeeded
in pulling it apart.

We watched together
as it fell to the ground
and smashed at our feet,
tears sprang to my eyes,
tears to yours,
each
separately
longing to undo the moment,
to walk backwards into the past,
to undo the moment,
the moments of pulling,
to walk backwards into the past
to the moment when
we could have shared
or taken turns
or something.

Come my friend
(for haven't we become friends after all
sharing our intimate
our primal pain)
come my friend,
come sit with me on the ground,
let us heap ashes on each other,
gently tenderly
I will teach you the melody
of my *Echa*,
together we will sit on the ground
and mourn for the peace of Jerusalem.

—*Merle Feld*

During the Assassinations

I took the cello to its lesson,
the cheerleader to the gym.
I was a sixties soccer mom

and when the bassoon needed
double reeds to suck on
I scoured Boston.

I bought red knee-highs for the cheerleader.
Skirts wide enough to straddle
the cello onstage.

Cacophony of warm-up, then
the oboe's A, *every*
good boy does fine, football

games with fake pompoms
siss-boom-ba and after,
gropings under the grandstands.

I went where I was called to go.
I clapped, I comforted.
I kept my eyes on Huntley and Brinkley.

During the assassinations
I marched with other soccer moms.
I carried lemons in case of tear gas.

I have a dream became my dream.
I stood all night
on the steps of the Pentagon.

With each new death
I added my grief
To the grief of millions

but always her pink suit
on the flat trunk of the limousine
and in her hand a piece of his skull.

      —Maxine Kumin

On the Death of Yitzchak Rabin

Old soldiers aren't supposed to die,
they're supposed to slowly fade away,
but ours is a new country, a small country,
and we must be parsimonious with everything,
even our old soldiers.

We cannot afford to retire our old soldiers,
we can't relegate them to corners, to rockers,
to retelling the stories of their glories
and their wounds.

We need them still on the front lines,
in the front row, we need them
standing up for us
while they have strength left to stand.

Even when we tear at them,
even when we curse them, piling insults,
calling traitor, traitor,
we need to squeeze all our resources,
wring harvests from parched earth, from desert.

We don't let go of our old soldiers, we shake
them by the throat, we choke them,
we make them cry, sinking to their knees
calling out for peace.

—Merle Feld

שָׁבַתֹ מְשׂוֹשׂ לִבֵּנוּ בֶהְפַּךְ
לְאֵבֶל מְחֹלֵנוּ.

Joy has disappeared from our hearts,
our dance has turned to grief.

Lamentations 5:15

Part IV
Rising in a Tent of Grief

Grief naturally stimulates reflection about what might be beyond this life. For some of us grief affirms that death completes each singular life—unique of itself, never to be repeated. For some it is an affirmation of a continuation that human imagination stretches to name. Some of us become less comfortable with God language; some of us move more deeply into theological frames. Grief reveals a spiritual truth: theology is inherently clumsy. The words we say expose a yearning that forces the depth of breath across our throats to express something that is ultimately wordless. The acts we engage in expose a striving to contain something that is ultimately boundless. Yet we need the efforts of our natural spiritual hunger to contemplate the awe of life, wherever it may reside: the landscape where both a sense of curiosity and a sense of caution naturally bring us to wonder about what lives or what continues, if anything, beyond any one life.

Kavanah

Creator of All, the universe is too large for me to fully know all that You know, all that You see, all that You hear. Even though You are beyond my own ken, I yearn for continued insight, continued guidance, continued relationship with You so that I can grow more fully into the divine image You have willed me to become. In my doubts of You, in my surety, and even in my unsureness, please support me in my continued journey to fold grief into my life.

And every person is a dam . . .

And every person is a dam between past and future.
When he dies the dam bursts, the past breaks into
   the future,
and there is no before or after. All time becomes
   one time
like our God: our Time is One.
Blessed be the memory of the dam.

   —*Yehuda Amichai*

K'riah — Tearing the Cloth

Why rend the clothes?
So strange to a tradition
that admonishes
not to break or to destroy

It is for the sake of anger
against the unfairness of the world
anger against him or her, God or self?

Is tearing the cloth to give outer expression
to the
tattered soul within?

Or is it a parallelism
the death of a person like the burning of a Sefer Torah
for which tearing the clothes is performed?

The burial of a human like the burial of a Torah
A human being is like a Sefer Torah
Studied, it has wisdom to impart
Lived, it has goodness to convey.
Rend the garments for the "Torah-mensch"

Each of us a letter in
the Torah scroll
Together our lives are intertwined

Our common fate and faith
our common destiny
find us like the stitches of the parchment
when any of us is lost
The holy text is torn.
In memory we are mended.

> —*Rabbi Harold M. Schulweis*

After Shivah

The days have passed
And a quiet has settled on my home.
My grief still holds me.
My sorrow is present.
Yet You, God of seasons,
Ask me to look gently
Toward the future.
You, God of Creation,
Ask me to imagine a time
When the pain begins to fade,
A time when my hopes are renewed.
You, God of generations,
Ask me to honor life,
To cherish memory,
To love those who remain.

Source and Shelter,
Loving Guide of the bereaved,
Lead me on the path toward
Wholeness and healing,
Peace and comfort,
So that I become a well
Of compassion and strength.

God of old,
Your ways are secret,
Sacred and holy.
You are my Rock.
You are my Lamp.
Blessed are You,
God of all,
Who redeems the bereaved
With love.

—*Alden Solovy*

Our Angels

Our angels
Spend much of their time sleeping.
in their dreams
they tear down the new houses by the sea
and build old ones
in their place.

No matter how long they may sleep,
one hundred, two hundred years—
ten centuries is not too much—
the first to wake up
takes the torch that has been handed down,
adds a drop of oil to the lamp,
blesses the eternal light,
and then recalls the name
of every other angel,
and one by one as they are remembered
they wake up.

For them
as for us
there is nothing more beautiful
than memory.

                    —*Howard Schwartz*

For the Bereaved

Rock of Jacob,
Comfort of Rachel,
Broken and torn,
Shattered and crushed,
Bereaved and bereft,
We declare Your Holy Name.

We praise Your gifts and Your works.
You are Author and Artist,
Architect and Builder,
Source and Redeemer.

We the mourners of Zion and Israel
Comfort each other.
We console the lonely and embrace the lost.
We cry each other's tears.
Together we recall Your wonder and Your majesty.

Holy One,
Ineffable Redeemer,
Guiding Hand,
Gentle Hand,
Loving Hand,
Light of Israel,
You are our Shelter.

$\qquad$ —*Alden Solovy*

Don't Let Me Fall

Don't let me fall
As a stone falls on the hard ground.
And don't let my hands become dry
As the twigs of a tree
When the wind beats down the last leaves.
And when the storm raises dust from the earth
With anger and howling,
Don't let me fall.
I have asked so much,
But as a blade of Your grass in a distant wild field
Lets drop a seed in the earth's lap
And dies away,
Sow in me Your living breath,
As You sow a seed in the earth.

   —Kadya Molodowsky

Torah Study

I had another one of those moments.
This time when someone was teaching
that you don't cook the meat of a baby goat in its
    own mother's milk.
That's where keeping kosher comes from.
I couldn't hear the rest.
All I thought was,
it's not kosher for a father to hear the earth fall on
    his daughter's casket.
What if we had laws about that?

       —*Rabbi Eric Weiss*

Shall I Cry?

Shall I cry at the last withered leaf of fall?
Or the lonely swallow?
Or my grieving heart?

Shall I mourn the past?
Protest the future?
Bury myself in these losses?
The leaving. The death.

Oh you sea of clouds.
Oh you curtain of rain.
Oh you silent yearning.
You arrive as messenger and guide,
Sent from the Source of healing,
The Source of radiance and wonder.

This soul cannot learn to love
In heaven, where only
The vast blue glory
Of light
Resides.

—*Alden Solovy*

Tattered Kaddish

Taurean reaper of the wild apple field
messenger from earthmire gleaning
transcripts of fog
in the nineteenth year and the eleventh month
speak your tattered Kaddish for all suicides

Praise to life though it crumbled in like a tunnel
on ones we knew and loved

Praise to life though its windows blew shut
on the breathing-room of ones we knew and loved

Praise to life though ones we knew and loved
loved it badly, too well, and not enough

Praise to life though it tightened like a knot
on the hearts of ones we thought we knew loved us

Praise to life giving room and reason
to ones we knew and loved who felt unpraisable

Praise to them, how they loved it, when they could.

—*Adrienne Rich*

What were You thinking?

God:
They said today that our lives are in Your keeping.
And still You took him now?
You took the one love that kept my life in its own keeping:
my time, my shopping, conversations, my fun.
This Yom Kippur I hope to hear from You.

—*Rabbi Eric Weiss*

In Sorrow

Ancient One,
Send light into this darkness
And hope into this despair.
Send music into this emptiness
And healing into this aching heart.

Air.
All I need is air.
A breath to give oxygen
To the anguish within.
A breath to give voice
To the howl in my heart.
A breath to set me free.

I am undone.
Crushed silent by sorrow.
Bereft by loneliness and loss.
Still yearning for healing.
Still yearning for love.
Still yearning for You.

Ancient One,
Send light into this darkness
And hope into this despair.
Send music into this emptiness
And healing into this aching heart.

—*Alden Solovy*

Pregnancy Loss

Dear God, Healer of the broken-hearted,
we mourn today, we grieve for the one who could
   have been.
We mourn the one
who never knew the secret kiss
that comes with Your sacred breathing.
El Rachum v'Chanun, God of mercy and graciousness,
we have loved and lost.
Ours is the grief of dreams turned to dust.
We pray that You have breath enough to regenerate
   our hope.

   —*Rabbi Nina Beth Cardin*

When Dying Is Over

When dying is over, a different kind of memory
    takes over.
Not the memory that is obituary.
Not the memory that records the past indiscriminately.
But an active memory that sifts through the ashes of
    the past
to retrieve isolated moments and that gives heart to
    the future.
That memory is an act of resurrection
It raises up from oblivious the glories of forgotten
    years.
Even the memories of failure, the recollections
of frustration and regret are precious.
Broken memories are like the tablets Moses shattered,
placed lovingly in the holy Ark of remembrance.
Memories are saved,
those immaterial, disembodied ghosts that endure.
What is life after death?
Pointers, ensigns, marking places
that raise us up to life and give us a changed heart.
Perhaps a life lived differently, better, wiser, stronger
    than before.
What is left after death? The life of the survivor.

—*Rabbi Harold M. Schulweis*

Moving On or Moving Forward?

Moving on means starting afresh, which, short of being an amnesiac, is a nearly impossible task. *Moving forward*, however, means venturing forth on unchartered territory, navigating the world without our parents, our spouses, our partners, or God-forbid, our children for the first time. That's hard, sometimes excruciatingly so. From whom will we seek wisdom or guidance or comfort or nourishment for body and soul, as we move forward? *Moving on* asks us to shed our past, but *moving forward* allows us the possibility of bringing some of what we loved along with us into the future.

—*Rabbi Shira Stern*

A Prayer When a Loved One Dies by Suicide

Why, God? Why did he have to take his life? Why couldn't I help him? Why couldn't he hold on? Why didn't You save him? Why?

How God? How will I recover from this nightmare? How can I exorcise the guilt: "I could have done more," "I should have done more," "If only I had . . ." How do I forgive myself? How do I forgive him?

Help me, God. Give me strength to carry on. Heal my anger and shame. Ease the burden on my heart. Teach me to believe that I am not to blame. Lead me back to life and hope and joy.

I know the pain became too much for him. Death was his only hope for release from his suffering. Life offered him no such promise, no relief.

Let him rest now, God. Free from all that haunted him. At peace, at last. Watch over him, God. Be his comfort. Grant him the serenity that he so longed for in life. Let his death be his healing.

Amen.

—*Rabbi Naomi Levy*

Optimism

More and more I have come to admire resilience.
Not the simple resistance of a pillow, whose foam
returns over and over to the same shape, but the sinuous
tenacity of a tree: finding the light newly blocked on
   one side,
it turns in another. A blind intelligence, true.
But out of such persistence arose turtles, rivers,
mitochondria, figs—all this resinous, unretractable earth.

     —Jane Hirshfield

Mourner's Kaddish for Everyday

Build me up of memory
loving and angry, tender and honest.
Let my loss build me a heart of wisdom,
compassion for the world's many losses.
Each hour is mortal
and each hour is eternal
and each hour is our testament.
May I create worthy memories
all the days of my life.

     —*Debra Cash*

Mourner's Kaddish

יִתְגַּדַּל וְיִתְקַדַּשׁ	Yitgadal v'yitkadash
שְׁמֵהּ רַבָּא,	sh'meih raba,
בְּעָלְמָא דִּי בְרָא כִרְעוּתֵהּ.	b'alma di v'ra chiruteih.
וְיַמְלִיךְ מַלְכוּתֵהּ	V'yamlich malchuteih
בְּחַיֵּיכוֹן וּבְיוֹמֵיכוֹן,	b'chayeichon uvyomeichon,
וּבְחַיֵּי דְכָל בֵּית יִשְׂרָאֵל,	uvchayei d'chol beit Yisrael —
בַּעֲגָלָא וּבִזְמַן קָרִיב.	baagala uvizman kariv;
וְאִמְרוּ: אָמֵן.	v'imru: Amen.
יְהֵא שְׁמֵהּ רַבָּא מְבָרַךְ	Y'hei sh'meih raba m'varach
לְעָלַם וּלְעָלְמֵי עָלְמַיָּא.	l'alam ul·almei almaya.
יִתְבָּרַךְ וְיִשְׁתַּבַּח וְיִתְפָּאַר	Yitbarach v'yishtabach v'yitpaar
וְיִתְרוֹמַם וְיִתְנַשֵּׂא וְיִתְהַדָּר	v'yitromam v'yitnasei v'yit·hadar
וְיִתְעַלֶּה וְיִתְהַלָּל	v'yitaleh v'yit·halal
שְׁמֵהּ דְּקֻדְשָׁא, בְּרִיךְ הוּא,	sh'meih d'kudsha — b'rich hu —
לְעֵלָּא מִכָּל בִּרְכָתָא וְשִׁירָתָא,	l'eila mikol birchata v'shirata,
תֻּשְׁבְּחָתָא וְנֶחֱמָתָא	tushb'chata v'nechemata
דַּאֲמִירָן בְּעָלְמָא.	daamiran b'alma;
וְאִמְרוּ: אָמֵן.	v'imru: Amen.
יְהֵא שְׁלָמָא רַבָּא מִן שְׁמַיָּא,	Y'hei sh'lama raba min sh'maya,
וְחַיִּים עָלֵינוּ וְעַל כָּל יִשְׂרָאֵל.	v'chayim aleinu v'al kol Yisrael;
וְאִמְרוּ: אָמֵן.	v'imru: Amen.
עֹשֶׂה שָׁלוֹם בִּמְרוֹמָיו,	Oseh shalom bimromav,
הוּא יַעֲשֶׂה שָׁלוֹם עָלֵינוּ	hu yaaseh shalom aleinu,
וְעַל כָּל יִשְׂרָאֵל	v'al kol Yisrael
וְעַל כָּל יוֹשְׁבֵי תֵבֵל.	v'al kol yoshvei teiveil.
וְאִמְרוּ: אָמֵן.	V'imru: Amen.

May God's great name come to be magnified
  and sanctified in the world God brought into being.
May God's majestic reign prevail soon in your lives,
  in your days, and in the life of the whole House
  of Israel;
  and let us say: Amen.
May God's great name be blessed to the end of time.
May God's holy name come to be blessed, acclaimed,
  and glorified; revered, raised, and beautified;
  honored and praised.
Blessed is the One who is entirely beyond
all the blessings and hymns,
all the praises and words of comfort
that we speak in the world;
  and let us say: Amen.
Let perfect peace abound;
let there be abundant life for us and for all Israel.
May the One who makes peace in the high heavens
  make peace for us, all Israel, and all who dwell
  on earth;
  and let us say: Amen.

אֶשָּׂא עֵינַי אֶל־הֶהָרִים
מֵאַיִן יָבֹא עֶזְרִי.

I lift my eyes to the mountains,
from where will my help come?

Psalm 121:1

Afterword

ANY EXPERIENCE of grief naturally stimulates spiritual reflection. This universal human experience is forever woven into our history by the traditional greeting to mourners: *HaMakom y'nachem etchem b'toch sh'ar aveilei Tzion virushalayim*, "May the God who comforted the mourners of Zion and Jerusalem comfort you now in your grief." This wrapping of personal experience to our collective history is our tradition's recognition that all grief yearns for a communal response.

In grief, our souls yearn for succor. The Hebrew word for "prayer" is *t'filah*. It comes from the verb *l'hitpaleil*; grammatically it is a reflexive form that is typically translated as "judging oneself." In the context of our liturgical tradition one may think of *t'filah* as any kind of honest self-reflection before God. In this way any effort, by formal prayer, a poem, a journal entry, or wordless cry, is *t'filah*. Grief can stimulate both familiar tropes of expression and spontaneous utterances that become known only in the moment they emerge. Grief reveals the clumsiness of theology, because we come to wonder so much about the nature of life that we engage more deeply the same eternal questions that fill our sacred texts. Our hope is that the words on these pages have offered a constellation of comfort—some clarity, some insight, some affirmation—and that this solace has guided the spiritual journey toward a renewed wholeness. We hope this journey has affirmed your place in our ancient and ongoing engagement with our sacred tradition.

While this book was not written to be read from cover to cover as one would other literature, it does represent the eternal desire to form a narrative that simultaneously speaks to each of us as uniquely created in God's image and as part of our greater communal conversation.

Whether you have used this book for inspiration at a glance or in a moment of deep need, we hope that when you close its covers, it has left you with a richer cultivation of your spiritual life, more deeply stimulated to God, Torah, and Israel, and that with these pillars of our beloved tradition, you emerge with a greater capacity for resilience.

Sources

3   Forgetting Someone by Yehuda Amichai from *The Selected Poetry of Yehuda Amichai*, translated by Chana Bloch and Stephen Mitchell. Copyright © 2013 by the Regents of the University of California. Published by the University of California Press. Used by permission of the University of California Press and Hana Amichai.

4   The Thing Is from *Mules of Love* by Ellen Bass. Copyright © 2002 by Ellen Bass. Reprinted with the permission of The Permissions Company, Inc. on behalf of BOA Editions Ltd., www.boaeditions.org.

5   Grief Arrives in Its Own Time from *Prayers and Run-on Sentences* by Stuart Kestenbaum (Deerbrook Editions, 2007). Used by permission of Deerbrook Editions and Stuart Kestenbaum.

6   *!?~ by Rabbi Eric Weiss. Copyright © 2019 by CCAR Press, Rabbi Eric Weiss, and the Bay Area Healing Center. All rights reserved.

7   Talking to Grief by Denise Levertov from *Poems 1972–1982*. Copyright © 1978 by Denise Levertov. Reprinted by permission of New Directions Publishing Corp.

8   After a Year from *Works on Paper* by Jennifer Barber. Copyright © The Word Works Press. Used by permission of the publisher.

9 It makes no sense for you to say that you are gone from *Of Dreams and Bones* by Janet Winans. Copyright © 2009 by Janet Winans. Used by permission.

10 Loss-Change by Rabbi Eric Weiss. Copyright © 2019 by CCAR Press, Rabbi Eric Weiss, and the Bay Area Healing Center. All rights reserved.

11 Rent by Barbara Leff. Copyright © Barbara Leff. Used by permission.

13 The Widow from *The Privilege* by Maxine Kumin (Harper and Row). Used by permission of the Maxine W. Kumin Literary Trust.

14 The Widower by Hafizah Geter. Copyright © Hafizah Geter. Used by permission.

16 Trees from *The Weight of a Soul* by Laura Gilpin. Copyright © 2008 Elizabeth Darbro. Used by permission of Elizabeth Darbro.

18 From Scratch by Judy Katz. Copyright © Judy Katz. Used by permission.

20 October 8th (excerpt) by Sasha Smith. Copyright © Sasha Smith. Used by permission.

22 On a Violent Death (excerpt) by David Grossman. Excerpted from David Grossman's Memorial Day Speech as it appears on *Haaretz*, April 14, 2018: https://www.haaretz.com/israel-news/full-text-speech-by-david-grossman-at-alternative-memorial-day-event-1.6011820. Used by permission of The Deborah Harris Agency.

23 When Will I Be Myself Again by Rabbi Lewis John Eron. Copyright © Lewis John Eron. Used by permission.

24 Practice by Rabbi Melinda Panken. Copyright © Melinda Panken. Used by permission.

26 Dinner for One from *Of Dreams and Bones* by Janet Winans. Copyright © Janet Winans. Used by permission.

132 MISHKAN AVEILUT: *Where Grief Resides*

27 My Mother Finds Her Way by Susan Moldaw. Excerpted and adapted from an essay originally published by *Literary Mama* (www.literarymama.com). Copyright © Susan Moldaw. Used by permission.

29 in the castro from *Alien Native Son* by John Selby. Copyright © Martha Selby Ellis. Used by permission.

31 Twenty-two Years Later by Jessica Greenbaum. Originally published in Issue #77 (December 2017) of *Plume* (https://plumepoetry.com/2017/11/two-poems-111/). Copyright © 2017 by Jessica Greenbaum. Used by permission.

33 My Dead by Ra'hel from *Flowers of Perhaps,* translated by Robert Friend with Shimon Sandbank (The Toby Press, 2008). Used by permission of The Toby Press, LLC.

34 Love Knows No Shame, excerpted from pp. 184–5 of *All About Love* by bell hooks. Copyright © 2000 by Gloria Watkins. Reprinted by permission of HarperCollins Publishers.

39 When A Man Dies by Yehuda Amichai, excerpted from In My Life, on My Life from *Open Closed Open: Poems by Yehuda Amichai*, translated from the Hebrew by Chana Bloch and Chana Kronfeld. Copyright © 2000 by Chana Bloch and Chana Kronfeld. Used by permission of Houghton Mifflin Publishing Company and Hana Amichai. All rights reserved.

40 The Weight of Absence by Judy Katz. From *The Best of the Bellevue Literary Review*, Bellevue Literary Press, 2008. Copyright © Judy Katz. Used by permission.

42 "I have planted you in my garden . . ." by Ra'hel from *Flowers of Perhaps,* translated by Robert Friend with Shimon Sandbank (The Toby Press, 2008). Used by permission of The Toby Press, LLC.

43 Separation by W.S. Merwin from *Migration: New and Selected Poems*. Copyright © 1963, 2005 by W.S. Merwin. Reprinted with the permission of The Permissions Com-

56 After a Sudden Death by Alden Solovy. Adapted from the original from *To Bend Light* (www.tobendlight.com). Copyright © Alden Solovy. All material adapted and used by permission of Alden Solovy.

57 The Life of Memory by Rabbi Eric Weiss. Copyright © 2019 by CCAR Press, Rabbi Eric Weiss, and the Bay Area Healing Center. All rights reserved.

59 Thirty Days of August from *The Stones Bear Witness* by Shulamith Chernoff (Hanover Press, 2006). Copyright © Shulamith Chernoff. Used by permission.

61 My Body by Carol Allen. Copyright © Carol Allen. Used by permission.

62 Epitaph by Anna Margolin from *Drunk from the Bitter Truth: The Poems of Anna Margolin*, translated by Shirley Kumove (SUNY Press, 2017). Used by permission of SUNY Press.

63 Anniversary of Death by Haim Gouri from *Words in My Lovesick Blood: Poems by Haim Gouri*, translated by Stanley F. Chyet. Copyright © Stanley F. Chyet. Used by permission.

65 Remembered by Rabbi Hara Person. Copyright © Hara Person. Used by permission.

66 On Losing a Baby by Rabbi Hanna Yerushalami. Copyright © Hanna Yerushalami. Used by permission.

68 Loss of a Young Child by Rabbi Eric Weiss. Copyright © 2019 by CCAR Press, Rabbi Eric Weiss, and the Bay Area Healing Center. All rights reserved.

69 Your Death Is Not a Onetime Event by Rabbi Melinda Panken. Copyright © Melinda Panken. Used by permission.

71 Another Country by Barbara Leff. Copyright © Barbara Leff. Used by permission.

73 Kaddish (excerpt) from *Kaddish and Other Poems: 1958–1960* by Allen Ginsberg (City Lights Publishing, 2001). Copyright © 1961 by Allen Ginsberg. Used by permission

of The Wylie Agency (UK) Limited and HarperCollins Publishers.

74 On the Home Front by Carol Allen. Copyright © Carol Allen. Used by permission.

76 For the Record by Judy Katz. Copyright © Judy Katz. Used by permission.

77 One Evening, Years Later by Judy Katz. Copyright © Judy Katz. Used by permission.

78 Hard Mournings adapted from the original in *This Grateful Heart: Psalms and Prayers for a New Day* by Alden Solovy. Copyright © 2017 by Reform Jewish Publishing, a division of CCAR Press. All material adapted and used by permission of Alden Solovy. All rights reserved.

79 The Scent of Grief by Rabbi Eric Weiss. Copyright © 2019 by CCAR Press, Rabbi Eric Weiss, and the Bay Area Healing Center. All rights reserved. The phrase "scent of fields," is a reference to *reiach sadeh*; Genesis 27:27/*Tol'dot*, in which Jacob, bid by Rebekah, dons pelts to aurally deceive Isaac as Esau in order to gain the blessing of the first born.

85 An Eternal Window by Yehuda Amichai from *The Selected Poetry of Yehuda Amichai*, translated by Chana Bloch and Stephen Mitchell. Copyright © 2013 by the Regents of the University of California. Published by the University of California Press. Used by permission of the University of California Press and Hana Amichai.

86 Please Ask by Barbara Taylor Hudson.

87 Time Does Not Bring Relief from *Collected Poems* by Edna St. Vincent Millay.

88 Shock from *Living When a Loved One Has Died* by Earl Grollman (Beacon Press, 1995). Copyright © 1997, CCC Republication. Used by permission.

89 Grief's Slow Wisdom from *Peace of Mind* by Rabbi Joshua Loth Liebman (Citadel Books, 1994).

90 Present by Rabbi Eric Weiss. Copyright © 2019 by CCAR Press, Rabbi Eric Weiss, and the Bay Area Healing Center. All rights reserved. Excerpt from Mary G. De May, MD, from *hear/say: Stories about aging, dementia, art and life*, a collaboration between UCSF Memory and Aging Center and Voices of Witness, UCSF Weill Institute for Neurosciences, 2017 Regents of the University of California, "Being Present", page 305.

91 Try to Praise the Mutilated World from *Without End: New and Selected Poems* by Adam Zagajewski, translated by Clare Cavanagh, Benjamin Ivry, and Renata Gorczynski (Farrar, Straus & Giroux, 2003). Used by permission of Farrar, Straus & Giroux, LLC. and Faber and Faber.

92 The Names from *Aimless Love: New and Selected Poems* by Billy Collins. Copyright © 2013 by Billy Collins. Used by permission of Random House, an imprint and division of Penguin Random House LCC. All rights reserved.

95 All the Names We Will Not Know from *Voices in the Air: Poems for Listeners* by Naomi Shihab Nye (Greenwillow Books, 2018). Used by permission of Naomi Shihab Nye.

96 Stones (at Normandy). Author unknown.

98 Tisha Ba'av from *A Spiritual Life: A Jewish Feminist Journey* by Merle Feld (SUNY Press, 2000). Used by permission of SUNY Press.

100 During the Assassinations from *Where I Live: New and Selected Poems 1990–2010* by Maxine Kumin. Copyright © 2007 by Maxine Kumin. Used by permission of W.W. Norton & Company, Inc.

102 On the Death of Yitzchak Rabin from *A Spiritual Life: A Jewish Feminist Journey* by Merle Feld (SUNY Press, 2000). Used by permission of SUNY Press.

107 And every person is a dam . . . by Yehuda Amichai,

excerpted from *Open Closed Open: Poems by Yehuda Amichai*, translated from the Hebrew by Chana Bloch and Chana Kronfeld. Copyright © 2000 by Chana Bloch and Chana Kronfeld. Used by permission of Houghton Mifflin Publishing Company and Hana Amichai. All rights reserved.

108 *K'riah* — Tearing the Cloth by Rabbi Harold M. Schulweis. Copyright © June 2015 by The Schulweis Institute. Used by permission. The Harold M. Schulweis Institute offers all congregational clergy a free copy of *From Prose to Poetry*. We are certain that this collection of Rabbi Schulweis' poetry will be an invaluable asset at life-cycle celebrations and in preparing sermons and *divrei Torah*. The book is free, a gift from Rabbi Schulweis' family and friends. To receive a free copy of the book, please go to our web site, www.hmsi.info, click on the banner tab "Contact," and fill out the form. The password is hmsi-BOOK. We will ship the book directly. We will not use this information for any other purpose.

110 After Shivah from *This Grateful Heart: Psalms and Prayers for a New Day* by Alden Solovy. Copyright © 2017 by Reform Jewish Publishing, a division of CCAR Press. All material adapted and used by permission of Alden Solovy. All rights reserved.

112 Our Angels from *The Library of Dreams: New and Selected Poems, 1965–2013* by Howard Schwartz (BkMk Press, University of Missouri-Kansas City, 2013). Used by permission.

113 For the Bereaved by Alden Solovy, from *To Bend Light* (www.tobendlight.com). Copyright © by Alden Solovy. Used by permission.

114 Don't Let Me Fall is an excerpt from Prayers by Kadya Molodowsky from *Paper Bridges: Selected Poems of Kadya*

Molodowsky, translated by Kathryn Hellerstein. Copyright © 1999 Wayne State University Press. Reprinted with the permission of Wayne State University Press.

115 Torah Study by Rabbi Eric Weiss. Copyright © 2019 by CCAR Press, Rabbi Eric Weiss, and the Bay Area Healing Center. All rights reserved.

116 Shall I Cry? from *Jewish Prayers of Hope and Healing* by Alden Solovy (Kavanot Press, 2013). Copyright © Alden Solovy. Used by permission.

117 Tattered Kaddish from *An Atlas of the Difficult World: Poems 1988–1991* by Adrienne Rich. Used by permission of W. W. Norton & Company, Inc.

118 What were You thinking? by Rabbi Eric Weiss. Copyright © 2019 by CCAR Press, Rabbi Eric Weiss, and the Bay Area Healing Center. All rights reserved.

119 In Sorrow by Alden Solovy, from *To Bend Light* (www. tobendlight.com). Copyright © by Alden Solovy. Used by permission.

120 Pregnancy Loss from *Tears of Sorrow, Seeds of Hope: A Jewish Spiritual Companion for Infertility and Pregnancy Loss* by Rabbi Nina Beth Cardin (Jewish Lights Publishing, 1999). Copyright © 1999 by Rabbi Nina Beth Cardin. Used by permission of the author.

121 When Dying Is Over excerpted from Life and Death by Rabbi Harold M. Schulweis. Copyright © June 2015 by The Schulweis Institute. Used by permission. See note for page 108.

122 Moving On or Moving Forward? by Rabbi Shira Stern. Copyright © Rabbi Shira Stern. Used by permission.

123 A Prayer When a Loved One Dies by Suicide from *Talking to God: Personal Prayers for Times of Joy, Sadness, Struggle, and Celebration* by Rabbi Naomi Levy. Reprinted by permission of ICM Partners.